FOR AS FAR AS THE EYE CAN SEE

Biblioasis International Translation Series
General Editor: Stephen Henighan

I Wrote Stone: The Selected Poetry of Ryszard Kapuściński (Poland)
Translated by Diana Kuprel and Marek Kusiba

Good Morning Comrades by Ondjaki (Angola)
Translated by Stephen Henighan

Kahn & Engelmann by Hans Eichner (Austria-Canada)
Translated by Jean M. Snook

Dance With Snakes by Horacio Castellanos Moya (El Salvador)
Translated by Lee Paula Springer

Black Alley by Mauricio Segura (Quebec)
Translated by Dawn M. Cornelio

The Accident by Mihail Sebastian (Romania)
Translated by Stephen Henighan

Love Poems by Jaime Sabines (Mexico)
Translated by Colin Carberry

The End of the Story by Liliana Heker (Argentina)
Translated by Andrea G. Labinger

The Tuner of Silences by Mia Couto (Mozambique)
Translated by David Brookshaw

For as Far as the Eye Can See by Robert Melançon (Quebec)
Translated by Judith Cowan

Robert Melançon

FOR AS FAR AS THE EYE CAN SEE

Translated from the French by
Judith Cowan

BIBLIOASIS

Originally published as *Le Paradis des apparences. Essai de poemes réalistes* by Éditions du Noroît, Montreal, Quebec, 2004.

FIRST EDITION

Library and Archives Canada Cataloguing in Publication

Melançon, Robert, 1947-
[Paradis des apparences. English]
 For as far as the eye can see / Robert Melançon ; translated by Judith Cowan.

(Biblioasis international translation series)
Translation of: Le paradis des apparences : essai de poèmes réalistes.
Poems.

Also issued in electronic format.
ISBN 978-1-927428-18-4

 I. Cowan, Judith II. Title. III. Title: Paradis des apparences.
English. IV. Series: Biblioasis international translation series

PS8576.E455P3713 2013   C841'.54   C2012-907686-4

Edited by Stephen Henighan
Copy-edited by Dan Wells
Typeset by Chris Andrechek

Biblioasis acknowledges the ongoing financial support of the Government of Canada through the Canada Council for the Arts, Canadian Heritage, the Canada Book Fund; and the Government of Ontario through the Ontario Arts Council. We acknowledge the financial support of the Government of Canada, through the National Translation Program for Book Publishing for out translation activities

For Charlotte

I

Snow, over roofs, and trees, and the ground,
in answer to the wash-tint that stands for sky,
is brighter than this inky light of day.

Between the post office chimney and
the radio tower, a pigeon's tracing
a hyberbole, erased behind him as he flies.

A wire-running squirrel has followed
the telephone line across to the maple tree,
of which he's exploring the ramifications.

One might search in vain for any other event
in this theatre reduced to almost nothing,
enclosed by mounting tiers of brick houses.

Between the buildings a bloated sun wanders
from window to window through a multi-storeyed
sky ruled off in glass and metal squares.

Sometimes a bird will hit this hardened
space, through which the far-off clouds parade.
The street sinks deeper into evening; cars

inch ahead in compact lines, stopping
at red lights that mirror the setting sun,
then beginning again their endless

caterpillar crawl. On the sidewalks,
the crowd trudges past under the sightless
gaze of mannequins in shop windows.

3

A cloud of newsprint birds flies up and off
across the square where night drifts down.
Soon waves of workers will be pouring out

in a swelling rush, more and more of them
from the subway station on the southeast corner.
A man wrapped in rags and crouching close

by the entrance to a tower built in a single block
of glass and metal, looks out of place with it all.
He sets a cardboard sign in front of him.

Cars pass, and a bus. Sunlight rinses down
over the cornices, runs from floor to floor and
reaches this man, weighed down by all of space.

4

A flock of pigeons sweeps down on the snow,
pecks at bread. This morning the park
is a rippled expanse over which the sun

sparkles too brightly for the eye to bear. Does
the soul retain such a blaze of whiteness? The
soul evolves into all that it has known; everything,

for the soul, is substance and accretion
as soon as a semblance of order appears.
Thus the trees become columns, holding aloft

the dome of heaven between walls of wind,
yet this temple collapses immediately
in a rush of unanimous wings.

5

Three birds you have no time to identify
fly through the leafless branches of the trees
against a backdrop of blue, of clouds, of sun.

The bells of a church summon you to noble
thoughts, but you do not pause for those.
A silent Buddha, sitting under a maple tree,

smokes meditatively while watching traffic.
A red dog pauses at the base of a trash can, sniffs,
leaves a few drops of urine and resumes his round.

You exchange a look with the contemplative
sitting on his bench. No doubt these tiny happenings
are written in him as well, and will be erased.

6

The books set out on the shelves, the sun
outlining squares on the table,
the bouquet of pens in a glass, a few pages

covered with a writing difficult to read,
crossed out. Beyond the windowpane,
the tracery of branches, the ranks of roofs

covered with snow, some brick walls, then
blue space for as far as the eye can see.
From time to time the wind lifts the red-

and-white flag on the post office. Some pigeons
go wheeling through the air. A squirrel runs
along the telephone wire, then disappears.

7

Above the streets, where there's nothing
but deserted space, the rising moon might
as well be an aspirin tablet, awash

in the sweep where the stars dissolve.
The stretch of roadway is covered in dust
with, here and there, some patches of ice.

It all seems hard and tight. How many can
be out at this late hour, and in such cold?
Only those few whose task it is:

policemen, ambulance and taxi drivers,
and others with nowhere to go, to be seen,
motionless, in the recesses of buildings.

8

We hear the cries of seagulls, which give
the city an ocean-front air, such a long
long way from the sea. Streaky clouds roll

through the blue expanse of foamy crests.
Missing are the whiff of iodine, the scent of seaweed,
but the wind's blowing from the northwest

insistently. If it were to rain, all this
would take on a thick layer of humidity
which would make the difference. We'd close

our eyes, we'd draw in deep breaths,
and that would do it; turning to face
the wind, we'd think we smelt the open sea.

9

At times there's a glimpse, down the channel of a street,
and wedged between two rows of houses,
of a bit of the river, like a fragment of sky

broken off and fallen out there below the horizon.
Some mornings, there's a lancing glint
or fiery gleam where the daylight's reflected

in its blazing mirror. It might kindle its flame
in anyone lost from afar to its contemplation,
but we do not stop for that; one glance

is enough to light up the heart, and those
whom we meet, a few steps farther along,
will not know where this joy comes from.

The old man stares at a fixed point in the midst
of space, where the rest of us see nothing.
The valley rolls to the foot of the nearby hill

which the autumn climbs in stages, a view we praise,
predictably, year after year. We're right, just the
same, to applaud all these yellows, these reds and

pinks contrasted with the pines' green, we're right
to come all this way to marvel. Above the grass
that looks almost painted and varnished, we seem to see

the air's transparency, washed by the wind last night.
Abruptly, the old man turns his back on
what he alone has seen, that we can never know.

II

Patches of light punctuate the landscape:
street lights, traffic signals, neon signs,
shop windows, reflections. Night envelops all of space:

housefronts engulfed in the dark, intersections
looking like islands, the air that seems
laden with soot. Above the buildings floats

a narrow crescent moon and a few stars stray
in the smoky sky's immensity.
Taxis drive slowly past, and other cars which

seem to be going nowhere, coming from nowhere.
A man sets down a vague bag of stuff in the doorway
of a shop, and stretches out in his weariness.

We walked along the river's edge to see
the night streaming, time rushing past
between the shores drowned in darkness.

The wind flowed, the air flowed,
the black that was all the immensity
of space flowed from every side.

We heard only the water, and felt as if
the whole of the dark was enlarging,
rising like a fountain and pouring back

into itself, into the redundant blackness,
into the rippling air, the fluid night and
into the river lashed with reflections.

A sphere of silence enfolds all
these stores we're walking past, crossing
by turns through blocks of shadow and puddles

of brightness falling from street lights
and shop windows. It's as if the air were filling
with vague rustlings, with fleeting

movements arising from nothing,
from whisperings. The signs blink yellow, pink,
and purple. The eyes of the mannequins

stare into infinity; it's a point somewhere
out there in space. They've been posed in
deliberately banal tableaux vivants.

14

Nothing is happening in the expanse
of blue, so perfectly blue, that has
stretched its canvas above the streets,

nothing but the event of the light as it
fades towards the horizon, diffusing
into a hemisphere without contours,

built up out of nothing. No sooner does one try
to focus on one point than the eye, lacking
an object, seeking in vain for something

to fix on, at once shifts back down
towards the broken line of buildings,
as if to rest against a parapet.

15

Night blurs the garden, opening it out
into a space through which one searches
for the geometry of the constellations,

as if some pedagogical heaven were
going to reproduce the illustrations from
an astronomy manual for amateurs.

But the eye cannot distinguish the points
that the mind knows are stars from
those other patches of light projected

by the windows of the waking down there,
twinkling at the rim of the horizon,
out beyond the formless expanse.

Here on this side, pink faces smile
with all their rows of perfect white teeth
from under helmets of blond hair.

Across from them, bloodied bodies are seen,
crowds in black and white brandishing
placards, and refugees lugging bundles.

Then there's a tank, a missile, an explosion,
or the head of a prime minister. A little to the side:
breasts and buttocks. Elsewhere: cars,

pastoral landscapes and wild animals.
Magazine covers establish the truth of
this world, by categories, for all tastes.

We see rising ranks of roofs, a framework
of branches which the late spring
has not yet edged with leaves,

the criss-crossing of the telephone wires,
some patches of snow...a whitish sky
raises its rampart up behind as in

those naïve paintings which remain superbly
unaware of the techniques of perspective.
We see chimneys outlined against

a pale sun and spills of undecided
shadow. We see the air's transparency,
and the hazy dusting of the light.

The day draws down. It's as if the sky
were emptying out and space folding up,
as if the light were crumbling away like

plaster that has never been painted,
that's neither white nor grey and
that's casting an overlay of damp.

Seize this hour, or rather this instant,
this passage rather, from grey to blue-black,
as if everything were hollowing out; make

haste to see this, which you will see once only.
Night wafts through the air, which seems
suddenly made of some thick substance.

Just outside the window, a redpoll
perches on a wire, preens for an instant
then vanishes. Sparrows, raccoons,

insects and spiders and squirrels from
the miscellaneous ark of our flood
haunt our streets, gardens and alleys,

although theirs is not the world we know,
our houses playing the role, no doubt,
of hollow rocks we come bounding out of,

dangerous animals whom it's best to flee;
as soon as we appear, they all fly off, scurry,
scarper, melt into the air, the earth and the walls.

Silence rounds itself over this landscape
formed of a patch of pale wall, a hedge,
a rivulet of grass and a few trees.

Windows stand out as yellow rectangles.
The night rises up. It's as if we could hear
the shadows spreading, little by little overtaking

the expanse studded with street lights.
Soon nothing will be seen but a rampart
of bricked-up blackness, compact and flawless.

Is this the disorder of a world's end?
The air carries stale perfumes which we quaff down
as if drinking swallows of nothingness.

All the light is radiating from the lemons
in the fruit bowl in the middle of the table,
which some avocadoes, pears and kiwis

enhance with green, copper and velvet patches.
Light falling from the window finds focus there,
everything arranged round this ideal centre:

the china cabinet, the buffet, the empty chairs,
solid walnut pieces, polished, almost black,
striped with reflections. The newspaper and the mail

are white and light-brown rectangular
patches, tossed casually on the corner, where
the cat has come and stretched out on them.

For all that, he's not so badly dressed,
and he's shaved this morning, this man
holding out his cap in the bus shelter.

He's mumbling a few inaudible words,
knowing that these people, whether they give or not,
have no wish to hear what he has to say.

All he needs is to draw their attention,
catch their eye and refuse to look away.
An old woman rummages in her handbag

and places a folded banknote in his cap.
Immediately he stuffs it into his pocket,
leaving only small change, which he jingles.

23

The light can be seen suspending
a hazy prismatic fog above
a long vista of gardens and

through a tracery of branches
that a late spring has held for
a month too long in winter nudity.

Its stippled shimmering lends truth
to the painting of Seurat; in a rosy,
bluish, violet dust, the luminance

clothes all these things with a
double that reveals, in philosophical
heaven, their shapes.

24

A fat cumulus cloud floats on a sea of blue;
it might be a sky by Poussin. It's much like this
that we imagine paradise—as an eiderdown

for us to roll ourselves up in while watching
all the earth go by below: rivers, valleys,
mountains and cities, and the oceans

with their toy boats, the forests, the animals
on the savanna or the tundra, better
than on television or at the movies, with

all the labours, the games, puerile and secretive,
of irreplaceable little men, each pursuing
affairs known only to himself.

25

We walk through streets we know
or used to know...the eye
collides with walls that were not here

when first we ventured out,
unwittingly, into this labyrinth;
a vacant lot which now we see only

in recollection, was over there,
where a tower of blue glass rises, a cube
of hardened sky. But a parking lot

offers an opening that lets us see,
at afternoon's end, the orb of a sun
which we are pleased to recognize.

26

In eight or nine hundred paces, we've passed
a dozen beggars, whom we have pretended
not to see. Farther along, a pierrot is sitting

on a folding chair in the middle of the sidewalk,
preparing his show—there's no way past him.
In his left hand he's holding a pocket mirror

and applying an ointment to his face, scooping
it with three fingers from a jar clenched
between his knees. Absorbed in his business,

he's indifferent to passers-by stepping round him,
amongst whom he'll soon find a willing audience.
Some of them, off to the side, are waiting already.

The light wavers through the window,
tremulous with rainwash. The whole landscape
blurs when one squints one's eyes, smoothing

the ripples of the water, unfolding the fluid canvas
woven on the pane by wind and rain:
a few trees, some grass, the tombstones,

the road over there, beyond the cemetery
and, farther off, tight ranks of houses
at the foot of the hill that blocks the horizon.

Then the light reaches the vanishing point,
towards that trembling in the west, that opening
into which the eye plunges and is engulfed.

28

By such a subtle variation in the rhythm
from the very first notes, which a movement
at once firm and singing launches

and withholds in the building up of an edifice
both unforeseeable and necessary, does one
recognize, in the sonatas of Haydn,

a world constructed of nothing but time,
from the progress in itself of a form that
seems the only possible homeland, and

which stands for everything: refrain and
variation, thrust and abatement in a slow,
measured impatience, at the centre of continuance.

We hear the wind gusting over the roofs
as if through a tunnel and, looking up,
are astonished to see so much blue, seeking

we know not what vault, what ceiling.
The earth beneath the changing sky
is an imaginary space. A dry leaf

that has clung all winter, falls. Tiny forked
flames, of a green shot through with yellow,
form on the lilacs, at the end of each branch.

In a maple, red and yellow tufts
are sprouting; thus the earliest spring
looks onwards to autumn. Time turns.

Space is enlivened at last with leaves
running along the branches' framework.
For too long this year the cold

has kept the trees in a dormant state.
This is truly the North; it's raining.
The low sky makes of the world one room

under a ceiling of vapours painted with
scrollings of chalky brightness.
Warblers, of the black-and-white sort,

fly down, perch, fly off and are gone.
The horizon lightens with a long pale scarf which
would have pleased the austere Glenn Gould.

A dancer carries the weight of the night
she's spent under the eyes of voyeurs;
a prostitute waits for her customer to leave

so she can grab a syringe; a drunk is using
a trash can for a pillow, snoring in the refuse;
under an overpass, dim shapes shift and turn;

a vagrant walks away, pushing a baby carriage
that he's heaped with his jumble of treasures; the
pink and green wave rolling and spreading

above the streets clothes them all in sanctity,
while those who despise them go on
sleeping behind their closed curtains.

Up there on a cordillera of clouds
the sun has set a glacier too white
for it not to be a fake.

Soon this sky will be leaden; there'll
be nothing moving unless the icy wind
(for this is the north, the North

of grey springtimes and the recordings
of Glenn Gould) starts a quivering in the leaves,
barely formed as yet, of trees stiffer

than fence posts. Outlined on the coppery
evening, the maple blossoms look as if
turned on a lathe, cut out with a blowtorch.

33

Soundlessly the evening burns, yellow-white
at the end of this unswerving street
bordered with a double row of trees,

and climbing the slope towards the west
between houses as rigorously aligned
as on a town planner's blueprint.

The shadows blur them all together until
suddenly this commonplace street resembles
a setting from Italian theatre, like

an infinite perspective in front of which
might be played out, in the failing light,
some tragedy in alexandrines.

34

The day has deepened into chambers,
corridors, porticoes and passages,
ever since summer has thrust up

partitions of foliage, raised up
hedges and woven the dome of boughs,
a palace with fluid doorways enclosed

in walls of light. In countless columns,
bearing their capitals of real leaves,
the trees support a blue vault

painted with real clouds, that move,
adorned with real birds, that fly,
and scattered at night with real stars.

The progress of sunlight along the wall
may be read as a sign the wind is rising;
it might be the glow of a burning house.

In the depths of philosophy's cave,
the shades whom Plato locked in must have seen
movements like these, so lovely.

The frenzied ballet of the birds suggests
they're announcing a storm, the first squall
of this summer so little like summer.

Heavy clouds jostle and bump along
a horizon suddenly solid as concrete,
then space fills up with a thick rain.

It all has to fit into twelve lines—a lesser sonnet—
all that's depicted at every instant inside the cave
dug out by Plato for the chaining up of those

whom he deemed to be dupes of illusion. But in his
system's sphere, the soul struggling to be free
had to swap for a stale whiteness, all pleasing things:

these wind-harrowed trees, the play of sun and shadow,
that pink-and-brown bird alighting on a wire.
So I shall settle for the paradise of what I see:

I trace this rectangle of twelve lines and
make of it a window through which to observe
all that appears, and that happens once only.

The sky behind's a canvas loomed from mist
and storm. The nearer view, of housefronts
in brick and stone, offers plain flat tints of

red, brown and grey, as in Breughel.
Beyond the rooftops we look down over, a slender
pointed steeple stands out against the light,

all depth lost. A fine rain, hardly more than
a dust of droplets, quivers in the air, while
colours, saturated, exude subtle seepages.

A man in a khaki raincoat, looking tiny
when seen from the sixth floor, walks
along a hoarding plastered with posters.

38

File folders, open books, a notebook,
some pencils, a floppy disk, an eraser,
a notepad, an ashtray, a pencil sharpener,

a paper knife, a computer, a ballpoint pen,
a packet of cigarettes, a ruler, a cup;
the sun splashes this jumbled arrangement

with patches of light, and its movement from right
to left marks the passage of happy hours.
Any table covered with objects randomly assembled

is a still life that could be painted or described.
Towards ten o'clock, a line of shadow will pass
across the dictionary, which contains all poems.

39

All that is offered at every instant: splinters
of sunlight, the sound of the wind, yellow,
rust-coloured, wine-red leaves, whirling...

on another day, under a hardened sky, there'll
be the geometric houses, etched with a chisel
into the eternity of an afternoon's end.

And reader, on the page, you will read what I
have before my eyes, what I set down in these words
and what I conceal in them, since they convey

only what you find here, what you put in;
if you consent, I shall not have counted their
syllables or pondered their meanings in vain.

A pair of sparrows hops across the flagstones,
showing off, parading their pale bellies,
their grey-capped heads and striped wings.

In syncopated skips, one after the other, they pass
from shadow into sunlight, that paints their feathers
with lovely brown and black splashes.

Their little round eyes miss nothing, ever vigilant
for possible danger, always close at hand: there,
in that bush, here, under this bench, everywhere.

Something has flickered, either a patch of sun
or nothing, conjured up by their endless anxiety
and, in a whirring of air, they've vanished.

At night, in the business district where,
a few hours later, a crowd will be thronging,
we can wander voluptuously alone

through a setting that seems nothing more
than simply false, as we follow streets filled,
at other times, with cars and trucks.

We can plunge into solitude and darkness
when nothing is left but the city's shape,
like a deserted stage.

All useless now—the names of the streets,
the billboards, the traffic lights—and the silence
of these new ruins lets footsteps ring.

We see the rain in the sphere of brightness
cast by a street light near a rowan tree.
We hear its ongoing whisper as water

patters over the leaves and splashes
on the roadway; we listen with pleasure to
its periodic murmur, infinitely reassuring;

we watch the endless weaving of the raindrops
through the air, over the roofs, the trees, the street.
The whole night is filled with its susurrus

which dwindles, then swells again, returning
like some inexorable trampling, soft-footed
and coming from all sides at the same time.

Places like this seem vaster, always,
at night. There's a sound of fountains
playing, spewing up streams of light.

The wind surges between office towers, then
wanders in the open, ruffling the ornamental
trees some landscaper has set out in an

even row to replicate the bank's colonnade.
Cars pull up at red lights, then start off
again with a noise of gears meshing.

At once it all seems theatrically
deserted, this setting of stone and glass
overhung by a cardboard cut-out moon.

44

Downhill, the city fades from view
under a watercolour sky, everything melting
into it where the horizon line should run.

Between the treetops in the nearer view,
through an opening found by stepping to the right,
is a dome floating high above the roofs,

which we see with matchless clarity through
the prism of a rain so fine that we divine it
without quite seeing it: almost an oscillation

of the light, an imponderable architecture
of reflections, with the fleeting beauty of that
which one will think one has not seen.

45

The narrow street climbs and turns under a thread
of sky edging in and out amongst buildings, hardly
visible enough to see what the weather's like,

if it's raining or not. Before reaching street level,
daylight here takes on the colour of the walls,
which seem stuccoed with dust and ash.

Once past the bend, reached with slow steps
because we're climbing a fairly steep slope,
and because this stern setting invites meditation,

we notice, through a vertical slit, the place
where a lake of luminescence quivers, source of
that rivulet of daylight we were following.

46

Lakes of blue are displayed between the treetops,
as calm as if they'd been painted,
as saturated as if they'd been squeezed

straight out of a new tube of acrylic onto
the sky's canvas, iridescent in the sun
and woven of air, light and water vapour.

It's no small feat, such chromatic purity,
at once transparent and stony as a *trompe-l'oeil*
on the vault of a baroque church, but one would

search in vain through this real, this empty sky,
for a saint's apotheosis, accompanied by the
swish of wings from a troupe of cherubim.

47

A truck rolls across the intersection
trailing behind it a bluish plume
through the nine o'clock light.

Wandering in the cool and limpid air
we see movements bereft of meaning;
they might be splinters of space,

or shards of light tumbling from the roofs,
as if traced by a cubist painter
between those houses, had he painted

this street, at this time of day,
in the newness of a world restored
to the paradise of its first names.

48

Between the trees, over by the cinema, we catch
sight of the sun setting a slow fire whose gleam,
beyond the park, tinges the facing houses.

After having gazed at its metallic splendour
through the gap the expressway opens to the river
(stream of mercury, haze of copper, fume of bronze),

we'll find its embers once again on a cornice
in a street the daylight won't have reached and
where it shows itself, furtively, only at noon.

For the moment we're strolling an avenue of maples,
like the country setting for some hermitage,
all golden, and scuffing our feet in the leaves.

49

A whorl in the third windowpane is
bending the landscape. Move your head and
at once the roof's edge pinches and folds,

at once the brick wall takes on
the pliancy of cloth, wrinkling and stretching.
And where does this game lead?

A simple bubble in a sheet of glass and
all you thought so solid is making a face.
To what serves mortal beauty? Hopkins asked,

and answered, too quickly, that it kindles
in man's mind the desire for what exists.
But look: it's nothing but a fold, or a knot.

A straight line between two fields of blue
is enough to make a seascape, minimalist,
but a seascape nonetheless if the observer,

whom one sees from behind as in Friedrich, adds
a little good will. Missing was the movement
of waves at the bottom, always the bottom, fringed

with the foam we've just added. With that come the growl
of the undertow, the cold air, salty, seaweed-scented,
the wind blowing from offshore, the scumbling

of the light in the heaving prism of the swells,
and this pallor in the sky, not so blue after all
when filtered through the spray of spindrift in the air.

The sun's taking pictures of the trees,
in black and white, on the sidewalk.
Projected on the ground and the walls

are copies of it all, swayed by the wind
and extinguished by the slightest cloud.
Thus there's a double lying beside you

whom you never glance at unless it's his snaking
shadow while you climb a few steps,
or else when a melancholy mood

reminds you that soon you'll be laid out
between his insubstantial arms
in an unending clasp.

"The bronze rain..." "No, it's a haze."
"The sun's bronze haze is announcing
that soon we'll be plunged into cold darkness."

"Not so fast—there's a choir of starlings
chirping in polyphony." "How can there be so many
of them (supposing there are) without our seeing them?"

"Never mind, we do hear them, and sometimes
too we hear the squeaking pully of a solo blue jay."
Close to the sun-warmed brick of the wall,

one feels a philosophical well-being, not
really inexpressible but certainly very sweet.
"It's not going to last, this artificial eternity."

53

In spite of the cars, the rain can be heard
pattering on the leaves and the roadway
in this mere murmur, devoid of melody,

or rather as a silence made audible.
The rain has no beginning. It seems
all at once to have been there forever

in a hidden fold of time. The passer-by
who's taken refuge in the doorway of a store,
looks out and around into blurred space,

slowly, as if seeking a glimpse of himself,
shadow of a shadow, shadow amongst shadows,
in some existence other than this dream.

Eighteen tomatoes have been set out to ripen
on the window ledge; the result is a
still life that could be painted.

The sunlight adds a rounded white
highlight to each of them, which is
balanced by a little pedestal of shadow.

Beyond the pane, a hedge plaits
a green tracery that provides a backdrop
blurred with reflections, over which the light

streams from right to left. Not even
the white frame is missing, or the silence
that consolidates this random pattern.

55

The sun just risen above the horizon lights up
a squadron of clouds that the wind is pushing
from the northwest across a swollen sky.

We've seen this spectacle a hundred times, on mornings
in childhood, seeing everything for the first time,
then later in photographs that stood for the world;

none of that stems our astonishment at such majesty
passing above a city distinguished solely by its
extreme banality. But we're not really seeing

that divine explosion of a world's beginning
(Earth, Earth, oh burning bush); we're watching ourselves
watching it, preparing to remember having seen it.

56

A revolving light flashes amongst traffic signals
in the street spangled with windows,
at the hour when offices are emptying;

it's some small drama, a fender crunched, not worth
so much as a line in tomorrow morning's paper.
The closed sky presses the night down

over this scene having all the appearances of the fake,
and which it is, irredeemably. What are you doing
here, walled in by so much shoddy stuff?

Darkness streams down across the windshield, swept
at intervals by reflections from the street lights, while
you drive down the disorderly street that is your life.

A wine-red sun smears the sky's canvas;
what a perpetually repainted ceiling it is,
this vulgar decor above the ashen streets!

We run up against intangible barriers,
we tramp through snow mixed with mud,
in the winter's chill, in the winter's drabness.

The soul does not aspire to eternal life;
it condenses into a breath or faint mist,
into a haze that thickens the light.

A crow splashes space with his inky shape
and, amidst the rumble of buses, performs
the solo part in a dissonant concert.

58

The sun's low circuit
daubs the housefronts with light that's pink,
white, then yellow, depending on the hour.

The trees no longer block its passage,
except with branches, boughs and twigs
that scribble their shadows on the sidewalks

in the thick or thin strokes of a writing
which no one will figure out.
By four o'clock the show is over;

the walls seem to lose all substance,
subsumed into the air as it melts into blackness.
In sum, another winter day is done.

A wall of night presses against the window;
we see nothing there but a surface painted
in the densest black, evenly, without a spot;

the pane becomes a mirror turned to the inside,
replicating the room while revealing nothing
that we did not see already, except that black.

It reveals no other space, only a fabric woven
by the absence of all light. It's refreshing,
this bath of blackness, as we imagine it,

not giving it form, the slick nothingness,
the truly limitless ocean where, for the moment,
one has no other face than this reflection.

60

A lilac strip, interrupted by the line of houses,
themselves enclosed by winter branches,
stands in for twilight in the windowpanes.

The daylight diffracting through the air's prism
has turned blue-black; as always it's
the same over-painting in the same pattern.

It's slathered with black, ever more
saturated, and keeps on thickening, blacker even
than anything Frans Hals ever brushed on;

it's clumping, covering everything,
patiently, not leaving the slightest chink
which might let us see we know not what.

61

The variations of the light raise up
a different city every day.
Fog, rain, snow and wind reweave

the weathered web of streets. Since this
is the north, the sun's a rare event.
At dusk, it's windows that checker

the broken horizon with symmetrical stars.
Then all collapses. The formless murk
heaps up its immaterial substance,

until a different space is shaped,
blind, cut through with close partitions
that fall away when one gropes ahead.

62

The expanse unfurled by springtime
spreads through the park and through memory,
under our feet and inside our heads—green.

We walk in the street, which the sun is
re-peopling with strollers, and in the idea
we create for ourselves of a street in April.

Moment by moment we move from the room
we fashion from memories, true or false,
to the heaping up of those tiny realities

that every instant's made of: the to and fro
of the traffic, the wind, the flight of birds
carrying augury only to those who desire it.

63

An endless crowd hustles through these streets
where even the cars, bumper to bumper,
seem to have come in search of gridlock.

Night's neons stripe colours over the jostling throng
and pour puddles of trumpery light on the sidewalks,
advertising the pleasures to be found within.

Perfumes mingled with sweat float on the air
between bodies touching as they pass. Little cries
are heard, and laughter and bits of sentences.

Eyes meet and shift, look again, seeking.
Some walk quickly on while others, furtive,
push in through doors that let out stale music.

64

Three geezers are lined up on the old folks' balcony—
or the balcony, rather, of the "seniors' residence,"
as the language of the century would have it,

to cover up what's really only a place to die,
where they shut away those whom we'll never see
grinning from the magazines' coloured ads.

Sitting in white plastic armchairs, as far
from each other as possible, without moving, and
rigid as tomb effigies, they may be dead already.

They're staring into the street's stark sunlight.
When we cross in front of them, only their eyes
move in their masks, and follow as we pass.

65

We hear, for the first time this year,
the long cry of the nighthawk diving into
the clouds of bugs that swarm round the street lights.

The room expands beyond measure with the
flood of murmurs pouring from the open window.
A car goes by trailing a rumbling backwash

that fades off forever into the darkness.
In this ocean of heat and humidity,
we shall not sleep without dreaming,

just as during the day we dream
that other dream, no less chaotic,
that's unthinkingly called the world.

66

The sun outlines the elms, the maples and
other trees out there, blurred against the light;
voices can be heard, engines, birds,

and the wind stirring in the leaves.
All this is part of evening's approach.
Clouds stretch a tarpaulin across the sky

washed by the storm at afternoon's end;
soon it will be paling, imperceptibly,
until broader and broader patches of shadow

are brushed across the walls, growing heavier
and heavier, till we see them painted over, until
black, unrelieved, will have snatched it all away.

67

This we read in a newspaper which smudges our fingers:
cosmologists have discovered that the world
is in accelerated expansion, or so they say,

into infinity. Lucretius knew as much as that,
and as little; from the fall of everything
in every way, all is done and all undone.

The sun in the wet grass lights up
as many stars as the eye can see;
a flock of starlings wheels, opens out,

gathers again and plunges into an elm which
instantly fills with chirping. The scent of newsprint
mingles with the odour of damp earth.

68

The boulevard runs beneath a sky painted
in fresco with a baroque landslide of clouds.
The alignment of the trees outlines a ship

surmounted by a perfect arch, rounded
above a colonnade whose capitals
of leaves and birds are stirring in the wind.

At the horizon, the slow rose-window
of a pink and green dawn glorifies
the rising of a sun so white it seems

the spectrum must have liquified within it.
Then all of space is washed with blue,
cars go by, and the day has dawned.

69

Try to recite the terrible names of God.
He's yesterday's paper scattering in the windy street,
and this faceless wind that creeps in everywhere;

He's a patch of sunlight on the grass in the park,
and that grass ruffled by the wind; He's a perfume,
the floating dust, that footstep walking away;

He's the cement of the sidewalk and the pigeon's
parabola between the trees and the roofs,
arcing unseen through the blue of the light;

He's the diesel smell behind a bus, those
absent looks you meet and pass, the prismatic air.
He's a word not spoken, which you shall never speak.

The man who walks at night, under an umbrella,
lends form to the world as he spins out the thread
of his promenade. To either side the street

is lustrous with the colours brought out
by the damp while, with each foot set down,
he pronounces a silent, ongoing *fiat lux*.

Each house, each tree, each passer-by,
the traffic and the spheres of brightness
that tremble round the street lights, are

at once erased as his steps transport him
onwards, into the cave encompassed by
the darkness, the shower and his meditation.

The sedum droops beneath its umbels which
the October sunlight tinges with pink and grey.
The sky, suffused with blue, is rounded

into a dome, its base festooned with cornices.
Crows—five? eight?—fly philosophically
up the street, all leisurely wisdom.

Suddenly, from an unknown source, and
irrepressible as the shower of notes in
a Scarlatti sonata, there wells up all the joy

that it is possible to know. Asters
splash the torrent of white light as it
shifts the shadow: the world's clock turns.

From the right, the sun outlines the edges
of this chair, tracing its anamorphosis
on the wall. Your shadow sits there, also

in anamorphosis. Your gestures, in that flat
grey and white world, are translated to the slant,
unless you yourself are the projection,

gifted with volume and solidity, of that web
of patches and lines moving on the wall's screen.
Unless that wall, those shadows, that sun, this chair

and you—this surface and its projection into space—
should open out, superfluous petals of no bouquet,
in a point purely ideal, at the centre of nothing.

Suppose that a gust of wind blows over the rooftops,
a single wave in the ocean of air, in the immense
openness of space, with no point of reference. Suppose

that the air is folding and rolling and that it's only
a noise, a rustling of the ether, the sudden unwinding
of a cable running out. There'll be evening also,

laid out in the ordinary street, between the houses
made of nothing, seemingly, but a slightly denser night.
There'll be darkness heaped at the feet of those houses,

and the channel of this street sunk deeper still,
where we shall pursue our course, step by step,
in the tides of the air and the eddies of the wind.

74

In this out-of-the-way neighbourhood, near noon,
there's nothing but autumn under a wide-open sky.
Patches of sunlight are redistributing

masses in the hollow channel of the street
under the tattered arch of a double row of trees.
The houses, slashed with zones of shadow,

create colliding angles. A crow, with
loud caws, takes possession of the world
from the top of a totemic maple, streaked

with straw-coloured and wine-red patches.
The scene is set for whatever event might
happen here, although the decor suffices.

Each house sends up a plume of smoke which
the wind beats back down on the roofs. In the
distant sky, shadow heaps upon shadow.

This is the year's lowest point, when nothing
seems likely to begin again, nor the cold cease
to weigh on the mind numbed by this allegory

that pictures its passing. But can the word
'cold' cause a shiver in he who utters it?
And can this city of concrete, metal and brick

be translated to metaphor? What is there
to decipher in these streets which the snow is
blending into space paved with greyish light?

The window squares off our view
of this landscape made of one angled street
and the contrasting levels of several walls

edged with trees plunked down, it seems,
in the most complete disorder. It should
be possible to render this in every detail,

on a sheet ruled off in lines, in keeping
with the example of the designer
of a plate which Dürer used to illustrate

his treatise on perspective. But it's all
laid out flat, with no vanishing point, on
windowpanes that also reflect the room.

A comic-strip sky, for some sunset ending,
unfurls violet banners above the street,
their contours sharp, on a ground as grey-blue

as if poured from an inkwell. The street,
almost empty at this hour, in this district,
leads straight to the narrow horizon framed

by two rows of housefronts. Two even lines
of trees trimmed back with architectural rigour
vanish in parallel. We walk through ideal urban

planning purged of nature and every irregularity,
towards we know not what, blissfully ignorant
but borne up by this perfectly oriented space.

A contralto voice responds to a clarinet
and we might wish the duet to last forever,
but as soon as the record stops, we hear

the myriad voices of the crickets through
the mid-September night, rediscovering time
and this rainy summer that never seems to end.

Of these songs one listens to with all one's soul
drunk with memory, dazed by what exists, and
lost between near and far, so that death,

we hope, may seize it in all ravishment,
which is the more beautiful? We cannot say,
in this dreaming dusk that is all of life.

79

You gaze at the window coated with black,
and striving to describe the city's expanse
through such a mild early autumn night,

you search for words that might raise up,
from a perfectly level horizon, the lemon
disk of a moon never seen except in painting.

For then volumes of shadow could be created,
with infinite space opening out between them.
But there's only this black, inked evenly in

and lacking all depth, but with, here and there,
patches of lighted windows, and the speckles
of street lights ... which everyone has already seen.

A driver stopped at a red light
sees the ages of life pass in front of him:
slender, supple schoolgirls, in uniform,

and old women alone, carrying bags,
as well as old men, just as alone, crossing
with slow steps. The street becomes an allegory.

Working people pass by, a couple,
a man walking a dog. All that's missing,
under a tree or in some recessed spot,

is a grizzled reaper with a scythe, maybe brandishing
an hourglass as well. The driver listens,
distractedly, to the five o'clock news.

A rowan branch looms up out of the fog
in which all else is progressively dissolved
like the background of a photograph when

the zoom, focused on the central figure,
drowns and dilutes the rest in light.
The rowan's vermillion clusters stand out,

lacquered with moisture, as incredibly clear
as if painted by Georgia O'Keeffe, although
she would have cut even that surrounding space,

grey on grey, where the light turns to haze,
and the knot of branches, a copper-green mass,
which is the single scrap of reality to be seen.

82

The October light is splintering
through the prism of the first frosts;
since it's freezing now at night,

the vegetation has taken on colours
that seem almost lacquered or varnished,
diffracting the sunlight in the streets.

Suddenly we realize that we're living
inside the universal clock, of which we
are only a tiny cogwheel. Red is mixed

with everything, the wind dumps it in the streets;
we catch ourselves dragging our feet through it
like a schoolboy whose homework isn't done.

83

A manuscript with crossings out, some books,
a few of them open, others in stacks,
a glass of pens, a paper cutter, scissors,

a ruler, a notebook, several pencils,
a pad of squared-off paper, a laptop computer,
an ashtray, a lighter, a packet of cigarettes;

all this would make up a still life,
unless you added—but he's here already—
a man, dreaming amongst these things and

facing an autumn landscape that fills the window,
which would result in another recognized genre:
the portrait of the artist in his studio.

84

Patches of sunlight on the blind,
mingled with shadows more or less dense,
produce an effect, as in the cave,

or on a movie screen, of a shadow of
something that may be only a shadow
or, as Plotinus thought, a chain

of increasingly tattered shadows.
The wind has cleared the sky of
the veil of haze that was clouding it.

We've raised the blind, opened the curtains
and gaze into an illusion of blue infinity
that stretches out and away, away, away.

85

Here on this side are the call letters PA
for Latin, and over there the letters PQ
for Romance literature, which is to say

for paradise: so much prose and poetry
that a blissful eternity would not suffice
for us to read it all, from Lucretius and Horace

to Saint-Denys Garneau, Borges and Montale,
from Aulus Gellius to Joubert, to Cioran, to Léautaud.
One could just as well say Seneca, and Ponge, and Leopardi,

Petrarch, Pessoa, Montaigne…one recites these names
and those of Sbarbaro, Erasmus, or Marteau, giddy
at having inhaled the inexhaustible catalogue.

86

The garden's chirping since a flock of starlings
swooped down on the trees around it.
There must be hundreds of them out there to form

such a resounding orchestra, endlessly
repetitive and full-throated, with amplitude
variations that are hollowing out space.

More reminiscent of Philip Glass than of Messiaen,
it's like a symphony with neither start
nor finish, made up of a single chord

sustained, layered, unfurled, as if flinging
an immense hurrah into the whirling
of the leaves in the autumn sunlight.

The wind scatters leaves into the light
while a flock of black birds passes over
in apparent disorder, but that's an illusion,

since all is structure without your knowing it.
You see the rain mixing a vortex of glimmers
into the torrent of sunlight, and you realize

that it's all music, moving and alive;
that this isn't a picture for you to gaze at,
languidly, at your leisure, but a great river

sweeping you away, and that it's this morning
in October, the first and last in all the world.
Your existence is not really important.

88

Pensively, a cat pads off down the laneway
between board fences enclosing small gardens,
crumbs or metaphors for that absolute garden, the earth.

Along cracks in the asphalt run threads of grass
whose pattern may spell out the inconceivable
name of God, or the shape of the world.

Busy with matters known only to him, the cat
sidesteps old papers, shattered glass, tin cans,
nameless objects highlighted by the sun.

We can't approach him; as soon as we step forward,
he walks calmly away, sure as he is of escaping
in a single bound should we try to catch him.

89

The fog pressing on the windows
adds to the silence in the house.
No car has gone by yet.

The city seems to be sleeping the sleep
of thousands of sleepers, each in his dream,
in his own chaotic, private world.

The newspaper hasn't been delivered yet,
the kitchen's raw light picks out each object,
even if night still lingers in the corners.

On the table, the basket of fruit is
trying hard, without success, to look
like the one that Caravaggio painted.

Let's lift our faces to this October sunlight,
and close our eyes; at once we'll share
the entirely philosophical well-being of the cat

who's stretched out in the grass,
unmoved that the wind around him is stirring up
a shifting edifice of perfumes.

Its brightness sifts down through the maple which,
in another day or two, will have few leaves left,
so that we'll see the bare bones of its branches

beneath the blue enhanced by clouds,
like a temple built of columns only, through which
a god might pass, what god we do not know.

The city's never so lovely as in the afternoon,
between three and four, with the day lowering,
in November. The light spreads, an ever finer

dusting of weightlessness over the stones,
with dim figures walking the dreaming streets
as they sink deeper amongst tall buildings.

Everywhere windows are lighting up. They cast
glimmering nets that may catch a face,
momentarily, then another, not as ghosts,

but seizing each in his singular eternity,
while the doorways of stores are lighting up
under shreds of sky whence falls the night.

92

All of autumn, finally, is only a sepia snapshot
with crackled edges, in which we see
some elms thrusting their branches' inky

strokes up against a troubled sky.
All of autumn, finally, is only a pack
of commonplaces, regrets for that which was

and was not, a wasteland swept by the wind
until, one morning, crossing the park, we feel
the grass crunch underfoot; it froze overnight,

and in the life-giving cold, in the air
that we breathe in with delight, suddenly
we know that winter's light is on its way.

93

Three men are tarring a roof.
Through the icy air we see steam
condensing round their backlit silhouettes.

It lends their movements that solemnity
produced in the movies by slow motion.
The winter sun climbs so imperceptibly

that time seems to have stopped.
We hear their voices when their work
is more difficult, but mostly they're silent

and we hear only hammer blows
ringing the sky's colossal bell
where the white light spreads and grows.

94

All is given at every instant in the space that
unfolds for the glance forever unwearied
of seeing what there is to see. One can begin

anywhere and follow the tremors of the light
beneath the sky's ever-present vault
where a cloud of birds is wheeling.

The wind shakes the shadows on the walls
still holding day's glow. Time does not pass.
It has never passed, since Achilles never does

catch up with the tortoise, since we never see but
that which is painted before our eyes: this street,
this rustle of sunlight blending into the air.

95

Through the rain, the leafless rowan tree
seems as if painted in stipples
that hint at its brownish-black lines.

The old masters knew how
to apply such touches, by means of which
reality might be recognized.

To left and right and out in front,
we see street lights and their reflections,
a sequence of patches the eye follows

in their random distribution through a space
furnished with masses that are sometimes
objects, and sometimes shadows.

96

The bread bag lies on the kitchen counter,
with the bread beside it, under the white light
that casts a round gleam on the tomatoes.

To the right, they're flanked by green patches of basil,
to the left, we see an onion, the salt shaker,
the pepper mill, and a bottle of oil.

This is almost a recipe, with the knife
beside the cutting board. On the table,
the basket of apples and plums makes up

a more usual design in yellow, red and blue,
although we are no less beguiled
by the same virtues of the frugal and the familiar.

97

A banner of clouds, the rising sun,
the point of view from which we look (a height
that lays the city out in panorama)

conspire to cloak the horizon in a canvas
painted with mountains we never knew were there,
like an Andean cordillera or the Himalayas,

of no substance other than the air, the damp,
the dawn brushing the rooftops. In the distance,
their lack of reality is not obvious to the eye

and we're inspired with a longing to deny
that these roofs and streets are realer, made of
harder brick and concrete than that veil of vapour.

98

All seems at a standstill in this quiet neighbourhood.
It could be Thursday morning, or the afternoon
of any other day. One checks one's watch. Outside

the grocery, an old woman sets down a bag of provisions
and looks at the snow that's blurring the light, a
prismatic dust falling from a sky where hangs

a sun that we can stare straight into.
Could we gaze at death like that, unblinking? Maybe,
if it was just as veiled and if it opened out

like this snow-softened day, like this space
where chimney smoke lifts and thins, like this street.
The woman collects her bag and crosses with slow steps.

99

Night has settled its simplest scene at the window;
red beacons from the radio tower flash the message
that the dark stretching out through the upper air

is an area of space that features solid objects,
into which one may crash, should one be a plane,
a bird, or an angel, and stray into this space.

Lower down, brick walls lit up by street lights
present a curtain cut through by angles and pierced
with windows in asymmetrical distribution.

Sometimes lamps are lit there and if, as here,
the curtains are not drawn, they offer the view
of a monad, enclosed between walls and a ceiling.

Northern birds are almost always in
the colours of wood, their feathers resembling
nothing so much as shades of bark.

The cardinal's an exception, so dazzling
you'd think him dreamt up by a hobbyist god
or drawn by a child who's just been given

coloured crayons and sheets of plain white
paper; he puts in a red patch, adds
a squiggle for the ruff, another for the rather

jaunty tail, and the buttery point of the beak
planted in the black mask. Then he crumples
the scrawl as fast as the bird blurs into the air.

The trees lift up the lightweight net
of their leafless crowns to the cloudy sky
that encompasses all beneath its arch.

There streams from it an even light, giving
all things their true colours; lacking the shadow
of darker tones to enhance the contrast

of their faces turned to the brightness,
this day swims all in the same waters, rising
and falling all together, all at the same time.

And what at first one takes for silence
is revealed as music, in such perfect measure
that we breathe to its rhythm, attuned to the whole.

Seize this winter day, under its demure and
fading sky, and this balmy-seeming air,
so warm is the sun on the grass in the park.

It should be covered by now. Only the snow
should smooth the sweep, which would
then be just as you picture nothingness:

devoid of qualities, and tainting even
the possibility that there may exist
the irreplaceable paradise of a single thing,

and one thing only. Do not indulge in imagining
a whiteness such as might bestow a face
on disappearance. That would be wrong.

The poet stepped up to the microphone
in front of the few people making up
the small audience that had come to hear him read.

In the bookstore window, before going in,
he'd seen his little book beneath a notice
which said "Sunday Poetry Readings."

He took a swallow of water, smiled quickly,
leafed through his book and hesitated to read the poem
that he'd nonetheless chosen when preparing.

He blurted out some words of explanation,
put his hand in his pocket, and then a different voice
was heard, which was and was not his own.

So much softness is a presage of snow;
the day has closed in, the air taken on
a scent of wood and of damp stone.

All seems to be waiting, motionless—
the houses, people in the street, traffic—
all displays itself, even the shadows.

We hear the cawing of a crow
and search for him in vain through
the fine network of small branches.

Then the clouds release, from zenith
to horizon, a downy light which
resolves itself, slowly, into flakes.

The waning moon above the fir tree
seems to overhang a landscape that bears
the name only because we have given it.

Landscape? The snow rounds off rooflines,
the snow does away with gardens, the snow
makes a halo round that moon. Landscape?

None of this resembles anything the word evokes.
This is nothing but a construct of faint marks:
some brick walls without windows,

the bluish humps and hollows in the snow,
a street light shining on nothing but branches
outlined with frost, and white everywhere.

We take another look at our invitation; yes,
this is the place. Through the windows, in fact,
we see small groups of people talking.

As soon as we're through the door, we're swallowed
up in a blur of babble. It's obvious no one
can hear anything at all. But that doesn't matter.

Being here is enough, being seen here is enough.
With a look, with a nod of our heads, we greet
those who wish us to see that they're here as well.

A voice calls for silence, there'll be a short speech;
the publisher greets the authors, who smile, and then
the din of voices resumes. This is a book launch.

The movement from night to day
and from day to night cannot,
in winter, be called twilight;

that should be a grander spectacle
than this imperceptible passage
from dark grey to light grey,

or from blinding blue-white
to the greyish white still giving off,
in full dark, a shadow of brightness.

All melts away with the hyperbolic restraint
heard in the playing of Glenn Gould
in his last recordings.

The junction of two zones of colour
draws a conceptual line, understood as
the meeting of two walls, at right angles.

At the bottom, an isoceles triangle suggests
the fictional depth of a space
made up entirely of patches.

On a trapezoid that stands for a table,
teardrops, circles and ovals are fruit
of a flavour which no one will taste

and flowers without perfume. A bee
that does not buzz forever approaches a rose
whose petals fall in dribbles of pigment.

A wave or tongue of snow laps over the edge
of the roof, which metamorphoses into white china
on which the insect one has turned into, crawls,

then flies off into open space, just as white.
Such was the dream or its setting. But one does not know
if the cat, perhaps a stuffed toy, that was sitting

at the window, or if the trial, which was about to begin
in a vacant lot at the moment when one awoke,
were connected in a linkage of cause and effect.

Or rather, one is sure of it; it all held together,
although it all crumbles very rapidly
as the familiar room resumes its shape.

Consider the disorder of your life
in the clutter on this table:
reports, minutes of meetings, agendas,

an ashtray, *The Tusculanes*, some pens,
a writing pad...the result is a collage
rather than a *vanitas*; what's missing is a skull,

an overturned goblet, an hourglass or a watch.
At the window, the sun's painting on the pane
in imitation of the illusion of depth

created by perspective, a landscape of levels
(streets, snow, roofs, the bluish air) into whose
vanishing you allow your eye to wander.

III

How can the moon, instead of a cardboard
cut-out, be an astral whiteness lighting up
the winter night like a different sort of day?

In the street, the snow scatters stars
through which we walk, which we can touch,
while from the windows separate worlds

shine out: the cosmos of each house
and of each partitioned room.
Snow covers the street and gardens

left to the wind that's hollowing out space.
The snow is impure, grey and shadowy;
lewdly, it stretches out beneath the moon.

Vertical strokes map out the space
and provide us with depth perception:
some chimneys, some trees and poles,

the wires stretching between them, the edges
of buildings enhanced by the sunlight
and framing a broken horizon line.

A swath of blue takes all the upper part.
A flagpole with its flag stretched out
lets us know it's windy, while the progress

of shadows marks the passage of the hours,
which a painter might render by varying
the angle of the sun, if he wanted to show it all.

The earth reappears as it was when we left it
at the end of autumn in the garden
which the snow was about to cover up.

We hesitate to walk there since every step
would leave a print pressed into the mud
where soon the grass will be springing up.

In a scant square metre, where archipelagos
of ice are pretending to be continents, we
observe the outline of another possible world,

with other seas and other rivers which
would need names, and which we might inhabit
as we do this one, under the same sun.

High above the cornices and chimneys
springtime's unfurling a sky of streaky
clouds splashed with the whole spectrum.

We've just passed the equinox, and walk
down the widened street towards the calm days
of the solstice, towards the schoolboys' sun.

A puddle left behind by March picks up
in pink and green the space the sunrise
is repainting earlier and earlier every day.

And in this mirror we can almost see,
between the cars misted with dew,
islands, and golden domes, and towers.

A wash of sunlight tints a concrete wall
uninterrupted by any window, any outcrop.
It can't be said that the sun colours it,

so delicate is its hue, it's hardly noticeable,
but at last we see it, this wall we've never looked at,
even if we walk right past it every day.

Later, we'll think back to its loveliness,
and the antique splendour that it raises up,
pink and peach, like an Etruscan tombstone in Umbria,

upon which we might decipher an epitaph—
because we've walked through a park where the snow
is flooded with the same ochre-tinted sunlight.

It's simply seeing what's in front of our eyes,
including the vanishing or collapse of everything
on every side: this theatre which we find

before us and around us, through which we walk,
tipping the horizon and turning the houses,
the walls, the trees, the grass and the street.

At every instant, it's all rearranged to allow
a complete event to take place; the air is painted
with sunlight, with damp, with dust; then

walls divide the space where a public bench
is placed, or a bus stop, or some signs, and
passers-by step in at once to play their roles.

The crown of an elm rises into the night like a big
broccoli; we see lawns perfumed with pesticides
under a half-moon that looks like a bitten cookie

hanging above the lines of streets; it's summer
in this city where, at this season, living is so sweet.
We hear lawn sprinklers, nighthawks and,

from a house converted to a Baptist chapel,
cries, because there's a service and the faithful
are speaking in tongues, or the Holy Ghost through them.

The street lights punctuate the humid darkness
with a double line of suspension points...
over that way are other streets, all just the same.

Between the piers a stretch of quiet water
resembles plaster on the point of setting
or lead on the point of melting.

Barges labour past, leaving wakes
that seem almost like furrows
in a soaked soil at the end of autumn.

Twilight touches them with golden flecks
which mirror and fragment a sky that
might have been painted by Claude, or by Turner.

Above the rampart of the buildings
that block the nearer view, domes, towers
and spires melt into the vanishing sun.

Children's cries rise from the garden,
an outpouring of joy such that it verges
on grief, the kind of laughter that might melt

into tears for nothing or very little, so
close does the pure joy of living come
to a sorrow without name or reason.

In the green, green grass, a ball
becomes a second sun, to be captured,
under the enormous sky where big

bellying clouds parade, and birds,
and a plane that's another bird
to be imitated, running, with outstretched arms.

The reader who's lifted his eyes from his book
perceives the sky above as the true ocean,
the immense expanse of blue enclosing

the whole earth, at whose end we might tumble
out of everything, should we ever find that end.
An enormous white cloud appears as

the crest of foam on a wave; it breaks and
streams in tatters while a pair of gulls fly through
the hollow space where blue ebbs and flows.

Before picking up the thread of the sentence
where he left off, this reader will have scanned
a summer afternoon's supreme iambic.

That's his cry we hear: *tweet-tweet-tweet-tweet*...
A cardinal's proclaiming his possession
of the street. There's no need to search for long

to catch sight of the scarlet patch he makes
at the top of an aspen; he's turned towards
the river, which we see at the foot of the slope,

over a factory district that the eight o'clock
sunlight is slathering, for the moment,
with the Arcadian softness of Claude.

As far as the horizon crenellated with towers
stretches a zone of rail lines and vacant lots:
his domain, soon to be buzzing with insects.

Ahead, always ahead, arises the day, the night,
the evening and, we imagine without proof,
that it's the same behind, that from this whole

a concave space is formed, within whose centre,
under a perfect dome, we settle in, arranging
the streets and their people all around us.

But it's never more than a screen, set on the retina,
with all the rest painted in. Quick as we turn around,
we never glimpse the nothingness that sinks away behind,

and which no mirror, a screen if ever was, can show.
Between the buildings the people press on, each one
pushing his world ahead, without looking back.

The stubborn bass of the crickets endlessly repeats
four notes that we hear through the humid night
at August's end, trying in vain to sleep. We listen

to the few cars trailing a rumble that swells,
then fades away, as a counterpoint of nighthawks'
cries enters in, or a distant siren, or footsteps,

or a breath in the trees, or the curtains rustling.
We hear other sounds too, confused and vague,
dreamt up in the slight delirium that arises always

from insomnia, but the true murmur of the world,
should one heed, even a little, its glorious orchestration,
at once covers over their too predictable monotony.

The rain arrives, familiar, expected, in an act
so close we touch the space that it enshrouds.
It descends like memory, green and grey,

forest, sea and street mingled in the cold light
that adorns each object with fresh details;
it comes nearer, repetitive, inexorable

as childhood was, with a rustling like the curtain
one draws at evening to enclose the room
and its swarm of dreams; it murmurs

a single word, repeated indefinitely, that
we cannot quite grasp, that we divine
or foresee, which is the secret name of time.

Sitting on the ground by the trash can, he stinks up
the subway entrance, calling out in confusion
to people passing, who know where they're going.

No one listens to his drunken, drugged-out
monologue—who could?—and no one
spares more than a sidelong glance for his

fumbling gestures, his pitiable efforts
to struggle to his feet, the looks he casts
at the incomprehensible mess around him.

He's a tangle of misery, a child of the slime,
made in the shape and image of their God, and
the police will shortly come and collect him.

As soon as the blind is raised, on which
only whitish rectangles were outlined
by the crosspieces, the landscape unfolds:

trees appear, the street, some zones of blue;
over the roadway is a tracery of branches
with the shadows of birds flying through.

Plotinus believed the eye sees only images
derived from inconceivable archetypes, but
the glance by instinct shuns the burning sun.

In the bathroom, when from the mirror's depths
we see a stranger looking out at us, we understand
that we're nothing but a knot, coming undone.

There's no better dancer than the aspen leaf,
its supple stalks the longest, the slenderest of the legs
to flicker in the green majesty of high summer's light.

From a distance, perhaps at the far end of a field,
an aspen looks to be fluttering thousands of flags,
like a strip-mall lot on a suburban boulevard

amongst expressways, motels, garbage dumps and lawns.
But that's beside the point, and a slight effort will
help us recover some commonplaces of the poetic tradition

such as *"lamp—the aspen is the lamp of the solstice,"* etc.
or *"a vertical river, a shower of reflections, a standing fire,"* etc.
But we prefer *"dancer"* or better still, *"the quaking aspen leaf."*

In the light of eight o'clock in the morning,
at the bus stop, people are waiting, lost
in thought and gazing at the sunlight

that washes down over the housefronts
on the other side of the street, and the cars
that go by, stop for the red light, and move on.

A woman clutches her bag under her elbow;
a teenager's beating time to the noises
heard crackling out of his Walkman;

a man's reading a newspaper and worrying
about rumours of war, to take place, it is thought,
a long way from here, in the evening, on television.

The blind's pallor hints at a clear sky.
It's never so blue, one never sees it so well
as at this season, through the trees' bare bones,

the light shining past unhindered by leaves,
of which there remain just enough to prick out
space with a stippling of red and yellow patches.

You do not raise this blind, not wanting the real landscape
(but what is real?) to cancel immediately
the one you are inventing. Then you give in...

and at once there unfolds, vast, motionless and blue,
the vista of the light, but which could not be painted
without an edging of shadows, and there are none.

What we see first is a stretch of rumpled clouds.
There's no white-albed angel passing through
amongst the birds, and therefore none is seen.

Lowering our eyes, we see the brick houses,
each at the end of its garden, covered
with the leaves no longer seen on the trees.

As for the trees, what we see are their branches;
they're joined to the upper parts of the trunks
by their branchings, appropriately named.

One might add the chimneys and the telephone wires,
but we shall not mention the wind; one does not see
the wind, and we shall speak only of what is seen.

We take a fresh look at the bark of the trees
now that the parasol of leaves no longer blocks
the light that's streaming down their trunks.

Under the sky's ruins, a colonnade has arisen
along the streets, and it leads forever
into the white dusk of November's end.

This is no temple, nor has it been deserted
by any gods who never passed here.
This is a neighbourhood with shops

whose windows offer fruit, or clothing; people
come and go; the air carries scents of pepper,
of steam, gasoline, moisture and coffee.

The window lets in the city's sounds
from near to far: hammer blows,
heavy machinery, sirens? some Varèse.

The expressway's far-off rumble stands
for silence, so little do we hear it. In the garden,
the birds are improvising on Messiaen.

Amongst the books, in a room organized
for solitary work, a reader is listening
to the buzzing of bees in the Latin of Petrarch:

"De remediis utriusque fortunae?" Antidotes
against the blows, either baneful or boastful,
of blind Lady Luck, whom no one escapes.

He was about to open that door, step into that room
where at last all would be revealed—when the reader
closes the book, putting off until later the rest

of the novel he's spent some hours with. At once
the characters make their exit, and a different,
familiar room rises up again before his eyes.

There's an armchair, a table, some other books,
and a jumble of all the things he recognizes:
a lamp, a sofa, a glass and a window.

These form a different dream, that seems real, perhaps,
only by a different convention. But who's dreaming now,
who's dreaming him, holding the closed book in his hands?

Strolling through the November dusk, at the end
of an endless afternoon, which is ending only,
is a chance to indulge in matchless delights.

It's not yet night; the brightness lingers
under a sky cemented above the streets and
over housefronts vanishing towards the horizon.

It's not day either; a grey and black fog
wafts up before our eyes as we gaze along
the row of street lights, lit up by four o'clock.

The stores are lighted; each window offers
a summary of the universe, and we stop to look,
with no purpose other than to savour time.

A few maples present an asymmetrical colonnade
unlike anything ever seen in Classical antiquity.
They're so much more ancient, one might declare

them entirely new, bathed in the light of beginnings.
But still…this is only a weekday morning
in the park that we cross on our way to the subway

and the noises of traffic will not let us behold
in this stretch of municipal grass the *locus amœnus*
of *The Bucolics*, or take ourselves for Tityrus,

even if, at the path's end, philosophically, a man
out of work is crumbling a bun into a pigeon ballet,
and eight in the morning is a point in eternity too.

Sunlight casts a spray of slender branchings,
crystals of light, into space as it dips and sways,
delicately, then opens out at the intersection.

One imagines oneself in panorama, set like
an exclamation point at the centre of the colours
as in Mirò—personage and point of view—

since one's watching oneself explore the stretch
that the eye invents on all sides. Then there
chimes in, like a symphony in a single chord,

the harpsichord of the starlings, the orchestra
of the traffic, and the perfumes, and the keen,
subtle joy sown by the shimmering brightness.

The houses leaning up against each other
offer a connected frontage of window rhythms
in the brick surfaces softened by the fog.

Sparrows clinging in the leafless trees
are fruit that no hand will gather; they
fly up and scatter as the stroller passes.

All he wants is to saunter down the slope of time,
spending at his leisure this afternoon of
a December so mild that everyone's amazed,

but as soon as he reaches the avenue, he'll act like
the rest, goaded by work and rushing from one line
to the next in the squares of their day planners.

"I realize I've got nothing to complain about..."
she says to the friend beside her
as we pass them on the sidewalk.

She's a woman in the street, plumpish, ordinary
no doubt, although we had only a glimpse of her
and will never know or want to know more.

It's enough to stroll in the light, in the midst
of all that it enfolds in its softness,
it's enough to be oneself a single note

and nothing more, in the concert created
by all these things, in this street, at this hour,
to have nothing really to complain about.

He walks slowly, limping, because his boots are
too big and blister his heels, and because he's tramped
for so long in the street like this, not knowing where.

He sees people stepping aside to avoid him, he guesses
they're turning to look as he passes, exclaiming at
the wake of stink that he himself no longer smells.

In both hands he's toting torn plastic bags that he'll
have to replace tomorrow if the trash can he's planning
to rummage in provides no others. He no longer remembers

not having plodded, lugging these worthless things,
through streets become one endless street, in the din,
the throng, the cold, the sun, the wind and the traffic.

The crow swoops and dips, wings outspread
under the misty sky. There have to be clouds,
between two seasons, before he'll appear.

He hangs in the air, seems to fall back,
catches himself and alights at the top of a maple,
where he sways, slowly and majestically.

The world around is made all of wind and cold,
out of the immense conch shell of space, the whole
laid out below, where he deigns to look down.

He inspects the horizon, of which he takes
possession with loud caws, then flies off
into the thickening mist, and is gone.

As soon as we step out, the cold stings.
The street seems hardened or tightened.
Space recedes in shrunken perspectives.

Instinct impels us, or habit, to pull in our heads,
and hunch our shoulders, to gather ourselves
together and offer less hold to the glacial air.

We hear nothing but the crunch of our footsteps.
An occasional car passes, underscoring
the perfect silence we're listening to.

Hard to explain what we're doing outdoors
in this weather, at this hour, absolutely outdoors,
and there's no one to ask the question.

In the vastness of a hospital parking lot (this is indeed what
the moon would be like, were we on it, quintessential suburb,
suburb of the earth), a crow alights on a lamppost

and loudly salutes the ten-thirty sunlight in its multiple
reflections on the hoods, the bumpers and the chrome.
Near the emergency entrance, ambulance attendants

smoke and gossip in the chilly air. They survey
the steppe of cars that they've seen so often.
A few patients shepherded by family, old people

or walking like old people, shuffle very slowly away
under the monumental sky. An ambulance wheels in,
lights whirling and flashing. The crow flies off.

You've got to tear up these drafts you've copied,
which are nothing now but the sum of the errors
and approximations that you've tried to correct,

although it's not without pleasure that you view the design
of crossings out, arrows, circlings, additions, scrawls
of blue or red or black ink, plus some underlinings

you don't remember making. For what purpose
do you study your mind's mess here, the random
chance that you tried to win—in vain, don't you see?

You were hoping for one true word that's neither here,
nor in those clean copies you slide into a folder and—
in their place—the just-about of your abilities.

I have built up a monument as fragile as the grass,
as unstable as the daylight, as fleeting as the air, and
as fluid as the rain we see running in the streets.

I've consigned it to paper that will dry, and
which may burn, or be splotched by the damp
with a bloom of pink, or green, or grey mildew,

and give off a pungent earthy odour. I've worked
in the transient substance of a tongue that will
cease to be spoken, sooner or later, or be pronounced

some other way, forming other words to convey
other thoughts. I've pledged it to the oblivion certain
to enfold all that this day bathes in its sweetness.

ABOUT THE AUTHOR

Robert Melançon is one of Quebec's most original poets. He won the Governor General's Award for Poetry for his collection *Blind Painting* and shared the Governor General's Award for Translation with Charlotte Melançon for their French version of A.M. Klein's *The Second Scroll*. A long-time translator of Canadian poet Earle Birney, Melançon has been the poetry columnist for the Montreal newspaper *Le Devoir* and the Radio-Canada program *En Toutes Lettres*. He lives in North Hatley, in Quebec's Eastern Townships.

ABOUT THE TRANSLATOR

Judith Cowan has translated the works of a wide range of Québecois poets, including books by Gérald Godin and Yves Préfontaine. She won the Governor General's Award for *Mirabel*, her translation of Pierre Nepveu's *Lignes aériennes*. The author of two collections of short stories, *More Than Life Itself* and *Gambler's Fallacy*, she taught for many years at the Université du Québec à Trois-Rivières, and lives in Trois-Rivières, Quebec.

FOR AS FAR

IN THE 144 POEMS OF *FOR AS FAR AS THE EYE CAN SEE*, Robert Melançon re-imagines the sonnet as a "rectangle of twelve lines," and poetry as "a monument as fragile as the grass." Impressionistic, seasonal, allusive, in language sharp and clean, this form-driven collection is both a book of hours and a measured meditation on art, nature, and the vagaries of perception.

AS THE EYE CAN SE

$19.95 CAD / $16.95

ISBN 978-1-927428-18-4

9 781927 428184

5 1 6 9 5